MASADA
REVISITED
A PLAY IN TEN SCENES

MASADA REVISITED
A PLAY IN TEN SCENES

ARTHUR ZIFFER

BOOK DOMAIN LLC
Publish to Perfection

CONTENTS

CHARACTERS

- » Decurion
- » Second
- » Essene Woman
- » Essene
- » Leah
- » Rebecca
- » Rachel
- » Husband of Rachel
- » Flavius Silva, Roman commander at Masada
- » Tiberius Julius Alexander, Roman second in command at Masada
- » Elazar ben Yair, Jewish commander at Masada
- » Josephus, author of the book "The Jewish War"
- » Mark, author of "The Gospel of Mark"

SCENE 1

At rise: Sometime during 70 ce, near the end of the Jewish War (66 ce -70 ce) between Rome and the Jews living in what is today the state of Israel. A Roman Decurion and his second in command are talking after the patrol that the Decurion commands has crucified an Essene in the region between Jerusalem and the Dead Sea.

SECOND: Decurion, all of our men have been killed. The Jews with their bows and arrows waited until it was light and then picked us off one by one.

DECURION: Are you sure all the men are dead?

SECOND: Yes I'm sure, Decurion, but the man on the cross is still alive. If we leave now maybe the Jews will try to cut him down and give us a chance to escape.

DECURION: No they will kill us with their accursed bows and arrows. I should have listened to you yesterday when you said that for us to stay here and wait till the crucified man died was a mistake. We could have made it back to our lines outside Jerusalem last night and been safe.

SECOND: Yes, we should have just killed the man quickly instead of wasting time to crucify him; and then we could have gotten back to our lines before dawn.

DECURION: Our orders are to crucify every Jew who tries to escape Jerusalem.

SECOND: But he was a skinny old man who claimed that he was an Essene and not part of the rebellion and was caught by accident in Jerusalem when the fighting started.

DECURION: Orders are orders. That's why I was promoted to Decurion and you not, because our Centurion knew that I would obey orders no matter what.

SECOND: And now we are going to die.

DECURION: Yes, probably, but I am not going to wait around to be picked off by some cowardly Jews with their bows and arrows. I am going to challenge whoever is out there to fight me one at a time with a sword. (He leaves.)

(After a while, Elazar ben Yair comes up.)

ELAZAR: Your Decurion was a brave man. He fought well with his sword, but he is dead. Now, if you help me get the man you have crucified off the cross, I will let you leave here and return to your legion.

BEN YAIR: Yes, I will help. I think he is still alive.

(They go and come back.)

ELAZAR: Well, you were right, he is still alive. But I need your help in carrying him to a place where he can recuperate.

SECOND: You mean you are here all alone. You killed nine legionnaires all by yourself.

ELAZAR: The bow and arrow can be very effective.

SECOND: You certainly proved that. But why are you here.

ELAZAR: I am on my way to Masada. I am actually going to command there.

SECOND: Then why are you travelling alone?

ELAZAR: On the way there, I wanted to see my mother; I like to be alone when I see her.

SECOND: But you put yourself at great risk, travelling alone.

ELAZAR: Yes, but it might be the last time that I see her.

SECOND: I understand. By the way, my mother is Jewish.

ELAZAR: What! Do you know that since your mother is Jewish that you are Jewish by Jewish law, even if your father isn't Jewish?

SECOND: Yes, I know.

ELAZAR: The fact that you are Jewish makes me glad that it was your Decurion and not you that came out to fight me.

SECOND: Thank you again. But I can't help but repeat how dangerous it was for you to travel alone. Look, we were ten; without your skill with the bow and arrow, you would be dead.

ELAZAR: That's why we Jews use the bow and arrow.

SECOND: We Romans prefer the sword and to fight in formation like the Greeks. By the way, I am an expert with the sword. It would not have been as easy for you to kill me with the sword as it was to kill the Decurion.

ELAZAR: Then that is another reason, besides your being
           Jewish, that I am glad we did not fight. But enough
           of this discussion, let's get the man down off the cross.
           There is an Essene settlement nearby. If **you help me**
           get him there quickly, he might survive.

SECOND: Yes, I will, but you have to let me go with you to
           Masada. I cannot go back to our lines alone; I would
           probably be executed.

ELAZAR: But are you sure you want to come with me? Masada
           is a strong mountaintop fortress, but you Romans
           will certainly besiege it.

SECOND: I know, but at least I will have the chance to die as a
           Jew. I have been thinking about this for quite a while,
           and providence has now given me this opportunity.
           Furthermore, if I go with you to Masada, I can help
           the men there to improve their sword fighting skills
           which will be needed against the Romans.

ELAZAR: All right, let us go.

SCENE 2

At rise: A few days later. The Second and an Essene woman are talking in the Essene settlement where the Essene from the last scene was brought.

SECOND: Hello, may I take the liberty of saying that you are a very beautiful woman?

ESSENE WOMAN: You're very forward.

SECOND: I have been waiting for a woman like you my whole life.

ESSENE WOMAN: I am an Essene woman and you shouldn't be talking to me like that.

SECOND: Why not?

ESSENE WOMAN: Because it is wrong, it could lead to cohabitation which is sinful.

SECOND: Who says that?

ESSENE WOMAN: The elders of the Essenes.

SECOND: But how do the Essenes as a group survive if they don't believe in cohabitation?

ESSENE WOMAN: By adoption of orphans, and by people joining our group. Also some Essenes marry and cohabit but only to produce children, not for pleasure.

SECOND: Then tell me, if you don't want men to talk to you, why do you show so much of your beautiful athletic body, much more than any of the other women here do?

ESSENE WOMAN: Do I do that? I didn't realize it.

SECOND: I'm sure deep down in your heart that you do realize it.

ESSENE WOMAN: Alright, maybe I do realize it.

SECOND: Do you know why you expose yourself more than the other women here do?

ESSENE WOMAN: I don't know, but I think you think you know and are going to tell me.

SECOND: Maybe you are not sure you want to live a life of Essene celibacy, and you really want men to approach you.

ESSENE WOMAN: Being celibate is not my problem, but I do want to have a baby of my own to love.

SECOND: So do most women; it is only natural.

ESSENE WOMAN: But we Essenes are supposed to resist nature.

SECOND: Not everybody can do that.

ESSENE WOMAN: For a Roman legionnaire, you seem very understanding about life and people.

SECOND: I might be a legionnaire, but I am also a person who tries to understand what life is all about.

ESSENE WOMAN: Now that we have talked a bit, I think that you are a very interesting man.

SECOND: Thank you. Do you know that I am going
                   with the man I came here with, Elazar ben
                   Yair, who will command at Masada, to train
                   the men there to improve their ability to fight
                   with swords?

ESSENE WOMAN: Yes I know.

SECOND: I know this is very sudden, but I don't want to
                   be the only man there without a woman. How
                   do you feel about marrying me and coming
                   with me to Masada, and there together we will
                   produce a baby for you to love?

ESSENE WOMAN: What did you say?

SECOND: I have been noticing you since I've been here.
                   As I said before, you are very beautiful; and, I
                   love you. Please marry me.

ESSENE WOMAN: You don't waste any time.

SECOND: I know what I want.

ESSENE WOMAN: Do you have a wife back in Rome?

SECOND: No.

ESSENE WOMAN: Swear.

SECOND: I swear that I do not have a wife back in Rome
                   or anywhere else for that matter; in fact, I have
                   never been married.

ESSENE WOMAN: Have you had many women in your years of
                   campaigning?

SECOND: No.

ESSENE WOMAN: Have you ever forced a woman?

SECOND: I never did. In fact, I never got promoted to
                   Decurion, which I should have been if promo-

tions were just based on skill and experience, because I was unable ever to bring myself to rape a female captive.

ESSENE WOMAN: How is that?

SECOND: My centurion said to me, "If you can't bring yourself to rape a female captive, then you are not fit to be an officer in a Roman legion."

ESSENE WOMAN: I find that hard to believe.

SECOND: In fact, once in Jerusalem, a woman captive looked at me with imploring eyes, to take her and protect her from all the other legionnaires who were going to rape her. I didn't do it. I feel very guilty about that.

ESSENE WOMAN: What would happen to these women captives who were treated so?

SECOND: Usually they were raped by so many men that they started bleeding out through you know where.

ESSENE WOMAN: What would happen then?

SECOND: The women would usually die.

ESSENE WOMAN: So how would it have helped if you had taken that woman who implored you with her eyes?

SECOND: No other legionnaire would have come near her.

ESSENE WOMAN: Why is that?

SECOND: From my father, who was a legionnaire, I learned the art of sword fighting from earliest childhood on. He was a great teacher and because of that, I was the best swordsman in my legion. No legionnaire would have dared to rape a woman that I was protecting. And by the way, my mother is Jewish, so that makes me officially Jewish.

ESSENE WOMAN: Yes it does, but what happened to the woman who implored you with her eyes?

SECOND: She died. I forced myself to watch from the beginning of her ordeal to the end. She kept looking at me all the time she was being violated. Was not protecting her what you Jews would call a sin of omission?

ESSENE WOMAN: I don't know, you should ask a Rabbi.

SECOND: If I asked several, would they all say the same thing? You Jews are always disagreeing with each other. Do you know why Jerusalem was destroyed?

ESSENE WOMAN: Because of Roman might, I suppose.

SECOND: No, it was the endless fighting of you Jews with each other in the lulls between our, I mean, Roman, attacks. Jerusalem was a very strong fortress and with your water sources within the city walls, the city could have held out for years.

ESSENE WOMAN: I believe it. I see how much antagonism there is between the various groups of Jews. As an Essene, I have had much hostility directed at me by Jews of other sects.

SECOND: Marry me, and I will protect you.

ESSENE WOMAN: But we haven't known each other for very long.

SECOND: Elazar and I will leave for Masada very soon. There is little time left before I will be gone; and, if you don't marry me now and come with me to Masada, we might never see each other again.

ESSENE WOMAN: Yes that's true.

SECOND: So what about it, will you marry me?

ESSENE WOMAN: Alright, I will marry you and go with you to Masada on one condition.

SECOND: What's the condition?

ESSENE WOMAN: That you become Jewish.

SECOND: But I am Jewish; by Jewish law, since my mother is Jewish, I am Jewish.

ESSENE WOMAN: I know that you are officially Jewish, but I mean I want you to start saying our prayers. You know Hebrew, obviously, since you can talk to me; it should be no problem for you to learn our prayers. And, by the way, where did you learn Hebrew?

SECOND: My Jewish mother made me go to Hebrew school when I was a boy.

ESSENE WOMAN: Then you must have learned the prayers there.

SECOND: Yes I did, and I will start saying them, now that you say you will marry me.

ESSENE WOMAN: Good. There is a Rabbi coming here in a couple of days and he can marry us.

SECOND: Can we start cohabiting now?

ESSENE WOMAN: No, certainly not until we are married, and then only for procreation.

SECOND: Were you conceived by procreation by your parents?

ESSENE WOMAN: Yes I was.

SECOND: Then after we are married, we can cohabit to have this baby you want so badly?

ESSENE WOMAN: All right, but remember only for procreation not for pleasure.

SECOND: What's wrong with pleasure?

ESSENE WOMAN: We Essenes believe that if we are doing something that gives pleasure, then we are doing something sinful. That's why, for example, we don't eat meat.

SECOND: I get pleasure out of eating meat and I need to eat meat to stay strong. Will you prepare it for me when we are married?

ESSENE WOMAN: Yes, but I won't eat it.

SECOND: That's fine with me.

ESSENE WOMAN: I think we understand each other.

SECOND: Another thing, what is this I hear about the people at Masada that they are mostly members of a group called "The Way"?

ESSENE WOMAN: Yes, I have heard that also; they are a strange group of Jews.

SECOND: Are they sometimes called Jewish Christians?

ESSENE WOMAN: Yes.

SECOND: There seems to be some similarity between you Essenes and the Jewish Christians.

ESSENE WOMAN: Yes, there is; both groups believe people should always do what they think is the right and not what they feel like doing.

SECOND: What is the difference between Jewish Christians and the people just called Christians?

ESSENE WOMAN: Jewish Christians are usually Jews who have joined the group called The Way, while Christians refers mostly to pagans who have joined it.

SECOND: Do we have to join The Way when we get to Masada?

ESSENE WOMAN: No, I hear that all Jews are acceptable at Masada.

SECOND: Good, I am going to Masada to teach the Jews there how to fight Romans and not each other; although you Jews at Jerusalem, when not fighting with each other over what seems to me to be minor religious differences, fought very well against us Romans. If the Jews there could only have fought as one, we, I mean, the Romans, would never have conquered Jerusalem.

SCENE 3

....

At rise: Some days later. The Essene who was rescued in the scene before last is talking to Leah in the Essene settlement of the last scene.

ESSENE: Thank you for taking care of me. I might not have survived without you. Not many men survive, who have been crucified, even if they are taken off the cross while still alive.

LEAH: You were gotten off the cross in time and brought to this settlement quickly.

ESSENE: But you took care of me. It was several days before I could use my arms.

LEAH: For a thin man you have very powerful arms and shoulders.

ESSENE: I have powerful arms and shoulders because I am a carpenter and that's probably why I stayed alive so long on the cross; I was on it for a whole night

LEAH: Not to change the subject too abruptly, but are you married? I heard that most Essenes don't marry.

ESSENE: No I am not married. Though you're correct, most Essenes don't marry. But you should know that. You are living here in an Essene settlement.

LEAH: Yes, I know. But I am not an Essene. I am here by acci-
           dent. I was in Jerusalem when the fighting started and I
           escaped. This was the first place I reached after leaving
           Jerusalem and now I am stuck here.

ESSENE: But you are alive.

LEAH: But I don't want to be an Essene. I want to get married
           and have children.

ESSENE: Then this is not the place for you to be.

LEAH: Yes, all the Essene men here belong to a group that
           don't marry.

ESSENE: Some Essenes get married.

LEAH: But I haven't been able to convince any of the men here
           to marry me.

ESSENE: You're an attractive woman. Why hadn't you gotten
           married earlier?

LEAH: In the past, when a man seemed interested in me, for
           some reason, I would not be interested in him.

ESSENE: Maybe you never found anybody you really liked.

LEAH: But I am a woman and should like a man if he likes me.

ESSENE: Oh, I don't think that's true. But I am not one to give
           advice on matters of marriage. Also, I belong to a group
           of Essenes that doesn't marry.

LEAH: But isn't the first commandment in Scripture to "Be
           Fruitful and Multiply"? Doesn't that mean to get mar-
           ried and have children?

ESSENE: I am not a Rabbi. I can't answer that question, but I
           am sure there is an answer. Not everybody wants to get
           married.

LEAH: Have you ever been attracted to a woman?

ESSENE: Well, yes, there were some women that I was attracted to. But I never pursued any of them. I am an Essene.

LEAH: You said you might not have survived without me after you came down off the cross.

ESSENE: Yes, I did say that.

LEAH: Then, in a sense, you owe me your life.

ESSENE: Yes, but then I also owe the man Elazar my life; it was he who got me down from the cross.

LEAH: I hear it said that you are going with Elazar to Masada to use your skill as a carpenter to make bows and arrows for the people there.

LEAH: Yes, I will go with him to Masada and make bows and arrows.

ESSENE: Then won't that be repayment enough for his saving you from the cross.

ESSENE: Yes, you could say that.

LEAH: Then how will you repay me for saving you when you were recuperating after Elazar got you down from the cross?

ESSENE: I don't know. What do you suggest?

LEAH: You can marry me.

ESSENE: What did you say?

LEAH: You can marry me. You owe me.

ESSENE: But I am an Essene.

LEAH: Have you ever had a woman?

ESSENE: You shouldn't ask me that.

LEAH: Please marry me.

ESSENE: What about trying to get that legionnaire, who helped Elazar bring me here, and who will go with him to Masada to teach sword fighting, to marry you? It turns out that he has a Jewish mother and is therefore Jewish.

LEAH: He has found one of the Essene women to marry him. Please marry me. I don't want to die without ever having been married.

ESSENE: Can I think about it?

LEAH: No, Elazar will leave here for Masada tomorrow morning. You have to marry me tonight. There is a Rabbi here now to marry the legionnaire and his Essene woman. He can marry us, as well.

ESSENE: Tonight!

LEAH: Yes tonight. And I promise that I will do everything in my power to make you happy.

ESSENE: Suppose I can't make you happy.

LEAH: What do you mean by that?

ESSENE: You know what I mean.

LEAH: Just marry me and don't worry about making me happy.

ESSENE: All right! I'll marry you. Let's go find that Rabbi.

SCENE 4

....

At rise: Three years later. Three women are talking on the last night after the Romans, after building a ramp up to the mountaintop using Jewish slave labor, have finally breached the wall around Masada and will be able to enter the stronghold the next morning.

REBECCA: The high council is meeting to decide what to do when the Romans enter the compound tomorrow morning.

LEAH: What else is there to do but just surrender?

REBECCA: A lot of the men would rather not be taken alive.

LEAH: At least they would still live.

REBECCA: No, then they would be crucified. We have held the Romans at bay for three years and they are furious at us for holding out so long, especially with the number of them who got Leprosy from baking three years in the awful heat at the base of this mountain, while we enjoyed the relative coolness of the mountaintop.

LEAH: Is crucifixion so much more terrible than being killed in other ways? Like with a sword?

REBECCA: Yes, it is a very slow and painful way to die.

LEAH: How so?

REBECCA: Your arms are tied to the crossbeam of the cross and your legs to the upright. When you hang by your arms, you can't breathe. Then you have to lift yourself up by your legs so you can breathe. But then your legs get tired and you have to hang by your arms and can't breathe again. This goes on and on, successively hanging by your arms and not being able to breathe and then having to lift yourself up by your legs to breathe until finally you can't lift yourself up anymore and you die, essentially of slow suffocation.

RACHEL: Now I understand why the Romans break the legs of somebody they have crucified if they want to speed up the dying. But it is a horrible way to die. Why are the Romans so cruel?

REBECCA: They are usually only cruel to people who rebel. And they consider our defense here at Masada as rebellion.

LEAH: So what are the men planning to do and what about the women and children?

REBECCA: The men feel, that rather than let their children be sold as slaves to die slowly working in Roman mines and the women raped repeatedly until they are dead, that each man must put away his wife and children first, and then a group of ten of the men will be chosen to kill all the other men, and then one of the ten chosen to kill the other nine, and then finally the last one left kills himself.

LEAH: But isn't there a Jewish saying "To Life."

REBECCA: Would you rather die slowly in agony or quickly?

LEAH: I just don't want to die.

REBECCA: You might not have that choice.

LEAH: I'd kill my husband before I'd let him kill me.

REBECCA: That doesn't sound like you love him.

LEAH: Yes, that does sound bad; it's just that our marriage has not been a good one.

RACHEL: I think my husband would not kill me if I asked him not to, especially since we have no children.

REBECCA: (Looking at Rachel.) You're so beautiful; you might be lucky and have a Roman officer take you for himself. But you'd have to survive the initial Roman onslaught.

RACHEL: Yes, you're right. To do that maybe I could stay with the five orphans who hide in a cave? Has the high council decided what to do with them?

REBECCA: I have the feeling the high council will not concern themselves with the orphans.

RACHEL: Then to survive the initial onslaught, I will hide in the cave where the orphans hide and come out after it is over. Also, somebody should look after the orphans.

LEAH: (Looking at Rachel.) I have no children either and would also like to survive; maybe I could hide in the cave with you and the orphans.

REBECCA: (Looking at Leah.) You are not so beautiful as to catch the eye of a Roman officer. Would you risk being raped to death? There are so many Legionnaires who have been here so long without women that they would keep raping you until you died.

RACHEL: (Looking at Leah.) Maybe you could avoid that. I would like to have you join me in the cave of the orphans. If we wait until the fighting is over, maybe by then the Romans would be over their initial blood-lust and not rape us.

LEAH: (Looking at Rachel.) And I would come out of the cave after you, when the Romans might be so transfixed by your beauty, that they would ignore me.

REBECCA: (Looking at Leah.) Would you run the risk of being raped to death?

LEAH: I don't know. I have something to tell you both.

RACHEL: Some secret you have. We all have our secrets.

LEAH: I have never been really sexually satisfied by my husband.

REBECCA: And whose fault is that?

LEAH: My husband is an Essene and doesn't approve of sexual intercourse.

RACHEL: But not all Essenes are like that.

LEAH: I know, but my husband is a member of an Essene group that thinks that sexual intercourse is sinful and should be done only for procreation, not for pleasure, and he behaves accordingly.

REBECCA: Than how come you married him?

LEAH: I was getting old and men were not looking at me anymore like they used to, and I begged him to marry me and he agreed.

REBECCA: Has he tried to sexually satisfy you?

LEAH: He has tried, but it has never worked.

REBECCA: Why is he up here in this stronghold, if he is an Essene?

LEAH: During the fighting in Jerusalem, he tried to leave the city and was captured by a Roman patrol. They tried to crucify him, tying him to the cross to die. But our commander, Elazar, on his way here, came upon the crucifixion, and he killed all but one of the legionnaires in the patrol; the one he spared then helped him get my husband-to-be off the cross while he was still alive. Then they brought him to this Essene settlement, where I was, to recuperate. That is when we met and got married.

RACHEL: So he is here at Masada out of gratitude for his being saved by Elazar.

LEAH: Yes, and he brought me here to this isolated mountaintop. I told him we should not come here, that we did not belong here. But he insisted.

RACHEL: (Looking at Leah.) Isn't your husband the expert at making bows and arrows?

LEAH: Yes, he is. (Looking at Rachel.) And, since, as you might know, your husband is his chief helper, they will probably spend all night, ignoring us, making arrows in case there is any fighting tomorrow.

RACHEL: What do you mean, fighting tomorrow? What about the plan for the men to all die before the Romans enter the compound?

REBECCA: It seems there is an alternate plan: and that is that the men would put away their wives and children quickly so they won't suffer; but then, instead of killing themselves, the men want to fight and kill as many Romans as they can. They feel they could make it very expensive for the Romans

RACHEL: But what about being taken alive and crucified?

REBECCA: To avoid the horrible agony of crucifixion, each man will carry a short Sicarii knife and will plunge it into his neck to kill himself if he thinks he might be taken alive.

RACHEL: It is beginning to sound like they have decided to dispatch their families but then, rather than kill themselves, fight.

LEAH: It does sound that way.

REBECCA: I'm sure that they will fight.

LEAH: To get back to our previous conversation, since I told you my secret, what is yours?

RACHEL: I don't think my husband thinks that sexual intercourse is sinful, but I have never really been able to surrender myself completely to him. I try and try but it never seems to happen.

LEAH: Is that why you have no children?

RACHEL: Possibly, but I have known women who have never been able to surrender themselves completely to their husbands who do have children.

LEAH: (Looking at Rachel.) You know we are the only two women in the camp who have no children and tonight our husbands will be busy making arrows and will probably leave us to our own devices. Therefore can I presume that you and I are agreed about us hiding out with the orphans in their cave?

RACHEL: Yes.

LEAH: Then let us go now to the cave of the orphans.

REBECCA: Goodbye my friends and know that I see nothing wrong in what you are planning to do, and God bless you both.

RACHEL: God bless you.

LEAH: Yes, God bless you.

(They all leave.)

SCENE 5

At rise: Later that night. Elazar is addressing the defenders of Masada.

ELAZAR: Some of you could not bear to watch what happened this morning. Let me describe it to you. The Romans had captured a family, husband, wife and son that had tried to escape last night. The Romans then proceeded to crucify the husband, rape with a long line of Legionnaires the wife, spread-eagled on the ground. Then they cut off the hands and feet of the son, cauterized the wounds, and then threw him into a large frying pan which was over a fire. The son kept trying to climb out of the frying pan but with no hands and feet could not do so. His screaming lasted a long time until he finally died as did his parents.

To continue, tonight is our last night of freedom. Tomorrow morning the Romans will surely come through the breach in our wall. Should we surrender? You all know what will happen if we do. We can avoid this by first doing something tonight that is very difficult, yes very difficult. And that is, that each man must dispatch, yes put away, his own wife and children. This way they will die quickly and mercifully. How could any man stand by to see his wife and children taken away from him with the prospect of a horrible death awaiting them when he could have spared them this agony? After doing this, each man will then have a choice: if his grief over having killed his wife and children is greater than his desire for revenge, then he can die with his family. But I know from what I have been hearing from you, that most, if not all, of you will want to make the Romans pay dearly for forcing us to dispatch our loved ones. Now if a man wants to die with his family, let it be so. But for those of you, who want to take some revenge on the Romans, there is a plan to fight. Remember, we are in a good position here, are well armed, and are good fighters. We are especially good with the bow and arrow. We could kill a lot of Romans. With this prospect in mind, the high council has discussed what would be the best way to fight and have come up with the following plan. We start with a tight half-ring around the breach so that we can kill the Romans as they come through it and before they can get into formation. Further away, on the higher ground of one of the palace levels, will be stationed our best archers. This will include five women, who happen to be expert archers, and who have indicated that they want to fight with the men. They will be positioned there with their husbands who will be able to make sure that none of their wives will be taken alive. Furthermore, on that palace level, there will be stockpiles of swords, spears, and, of course, bows and arrows, as well as water. The most difficult part of this plan will be the retreat to the palace level when a signal is given. This signal to retreat will be given when the Romans break through our half-ring around the breach, and the retreat will be covered by our archers on the palace level. With the element of surprise, we should be able to allow a large number of our men to make it up to the palace level to continue fighting. Also, I want every man to carry a short Sicarii knife so that if he thinks he will be captured while still alive and then crucified, he can, if he wants to, kill himself. Furthermore, if an archer sees a Jew on the verge of being taken alive, I want that archer to kill him. This way we can deprive the Romans of crucifying any of our captured. We are the last stronghold of our people; and by what we do here tomorrow, we will teach the Romans what Jewish determination, or, as some say, what "Jewish Iron," is all about. So then I want you all now to go back to your huts and do what has to be done with your families, and then prepare for the Romans coming tomorrow morning. Finally, I want to give all of you the blessing of our one mighty and perfect God and thank you all for having come here to Masada. You didn't have to come here and I thank you one and all for that.

SCENE 6

At rise: Second and his Essene wife are talking in their hut.

SECOND: You know what all the men are doing now.

ESSENE WOMAN: Yes I know.

SECOND: You Jews are tough: To kill one's wife and children cannot be easy.

ESSENE WOMAN: You of all people should know why it is necessary. You saw a woman raped to death.

SECOND: So am I supposed to kill you and our child?

ESSENE WOMAN: Yes, if you want us to die quickly and mercifully.

SECOND: Are you sorry you married me and came here to Masada?

ESSENE WOMAN: No.

SECOND: But you are going to die young.

ESSENE WOMAN: But these three years up here at Masada, having a child and living with you, have been glorious. As an Essene I never thought love could be so important.

SECOND: So you love me?

ESSENE WOMAN: Yes.

SECOND: As much as I love you.

ESSENE WOMAN: I love you almost as much as I love our child.

SECOND: That's to be expected.

ESSENE WOMAN: No matter what happens, I am glad I came here with you.

SECOND: Thank you for saying that.

ESSENE WOMAN: Did you mind giving up meat here at Masada, which you said you love?

SECOND: No, I quickly got used to it, and it seems not to be necessary to eat meat to stay strong.

ESSENE WOMAN: To get to something more important than meat, you've made the men here at Masada as expert with the sword as they are with the bow and arrow. Tomorrow when the Roman break through they are in for a surprise. You did a great thing and I am so glad to have been instrumental in helping you do this by making it easy for you to come to Masada.

SECOND: Yes, you made it easy for me to live here, but I must say that you Jews were apt pupils.

ESSENE WOMAN: Don't say you Jews. You are as much a Jew as anybody here. Your mother is Jewish, so you are officially Jewish. But more than that, you live as a Jew, and therefore you are Jewish if you want to be.

SECOND: Again, thank you for saying that. But tell me why are we up here. Why did the people here allow themselves to be trapped up here on this mountaintop?

ESSENE WOMAN: I've wondered about that myself.

SECOND: And also who is that old man living apart in one of the palaces with his family who keep to themselves? I have a feeling that everyone is here to protect him.

ESSENE WOMAN: Since we are not members of The Way, none of the other people here at Masada would ever tell me anything about him, except that he was an important person in The Way, somehow connected with the founding of the movement.

SECOND: Should we have become members of The Way?

ESSENE WOMAN: It wouldn't make any difference now.

SECOND: Don't you want to know what we are going to die for?

ESSENE WOMAN: It would help, but we are still going to die.

SECOND: You know, I have an idea on how we can survive.

ESSENE WOMAN: Oh, why don't you tell me?

SECOND: You, I, and our child, go down the Snake Path which the Romans don't guard, since it is so difficult a descent, and then make it to the camp of the Jewish slaves that built the ramp up to here, hopefully unnoticed by the Romans.

ESSENE WOMAN: And then what?

SECOND: After Masada is taken, the Romans will probably just disband the slave camp, since the slaves there were not involved in any rebellious activities, and let them fend for themselves; and then we can go to some Essene village.

ESSENE WOMAN: Would we go down the Snake Path by ourselves?

SECOND: Yes.

ESSENE WOMAN: Why can't we take others with us?

SECOND: Firstly, only a small group, namely, we three, with me carrying our child, could do it without making noise and attracting the attention of the Romans; and, secondly, of all the women in the compound, very few have your physical capability to climb down the difficult Snake Path; and, finally, the people here are mostly members of The Way and would not leave Elazar and that secretive old man they are here to protect.

ESSENE WOMAN: When would we go?

SECOND: Soon; in fact, we should go shortly after I say goodbye to a few people.

ESSENE WOMAN: What happens if we are caught by the Romans?

SECOND: You know what will happen. Are you willing to risk it?

ESSENE WOMAN: Yes.

SECOND: Then let us prepare to go.

SCENE 7

At rise: Still later that night. The Essene and the husband of Rachel are talking.

ESSENE: Well, we are finished with what we had to do. We have distributed all the arrows we made and have built ourselves a little perch on the highest level of this palace where we can look down on everybody. We should be able to kill a lot of Romans.

HUSBAND: This is a good idea. We can shoot our long bows from here and very few Romans will be able to shoot back. Now, not to change the subject, should we worry about our wives?

ESSENE: No. They know where we are and would come to us if they wanted to. But I am still worried about the five orphans. Are we doing the right thing by ignoring them?

HUSBAND: Did you speak to Elazar about them?

ESSENE: Yes I did, and he said that the high council had decided that only parents of children have the right to kill them, so the orphans will not be dispatched like the other children.

HUSBAND: Maybe our two wives, who have seemed to disappear, will take care of them.

ESSENE: Yes, I think I overheard some talk about them staying in the cave where the orphans hide out.

HUSBAND: Good. I would hate for the orphans to just be ignored.

ESSENE: But let us talk about what is going to happen tomorrow. The Romans will enter the compound, probably at dawn. With our long bows we should be able to kill anyone coming through the breach. We should especially try to kill any officers that we see and also anyone wearing a vest, since our arrows fired from a long bow can pierce a vest.

HUSBAND: It is interesting that we two are up here together: both of us have no children and it seems that neither of us will have to kill his wife.

ESSENE: Yes that is interesting.

HUSBAND: Do you have any doubts about us killing Romans? It does say in scripture, "Thou Shalt not Kill."

ESSENE: I have no problem with killing Romans. They could just ignore us on this mountaintop. We are no threat to them. Also scripture says that killing is allowable under certain circumstances. Certainly, self-defense is one of the circumstances.

HUSBAND: How do you feel about suicide in order to avoid being taken alive and crucified?

ESSENE: I have no problem with that. Crucifixion is a horrible way to die and, as you may know, I was almost crucified three years ago.

HUSBAND: You know that I am a Jewish Christian and, to some of us, suicide is considered a sin.

ESSENE: If you want, I can try to kill you and not let the Romans take you alive.

HUSBAND: Yes I'd like that, if it is at all possible.

ESSENE: You know, part of our mission up here is to make sure that no Jew is taken alive. That means if we see that a Jew is going to be captured while still alive that we should kill him. Are you going to be able to do that?

HUSBAND: Yes although, I would find it easier to kill Romans.

ESSENE: I'll tell you what: you focus on killing Romans and I'll worry about killing captured Jews.

HUSBAND: Thank you. Do you wonder if, even though that legionnaire whom Elazar brought with him and who has spent the last three years training our men in the niceties of swordplay, our men will do well in actual sword combat?

ESSENE: Yes. I think the Romans will find that we are as good with the sword as they are. By the way, did you hear that the legionnaire will leave the compound later tonight with his wife and child and go down the Snake Path hoping, with his knowledge of a Roman camp, to get to the camp of the Jewish slaves, whom the Romans used to build the ramp up to here, to hide away in that camp and possibly stand a good chance of surviving?

HUSBAND: Yes, I have heard that, but if he is captured he will be crucified.

ESSENE: Yes, but he says that he will make it costly for the Romans as long as he has his sword.

HUSBAND: He is a good man and I hope his plan works. By the way, do you find it interesting that our two wives have become so close?

ESSENE: It was to be expected since they are the only women up here who have no children.

HUSBAND: I have a confession to make.

ESSENE: You don't have to confess to me.

HUSBAND: I want to.

ESSENE: All right go ahead.

HUSBAND: I could never really make my wife happy sexually.

ESSENE: Maybe it wasn't your fault.

HUSBAND: Yes. She married me too quickly. She was very anxious to get out of her parent's house. Her mother couldn't wait for her to get married.

ESSENE: Do you know why?

HUSBAND: I think it was because her father couldn't stop staring at her, probably because she is so beautiful; and that made his wife, her mother, very angry. She, my wife-to-be, realized this and she married at her first opportunity, which turned out to be me, to get out of her parent's house.

ESSENE: But you are so well-matched. She is one of the most beautiful women in the compound and you're a very handsome man, if I can say that without embarrassing you.

HUSBAND: Are you saying she married me because of my appearance, and that she really didn't love me?

ESSENE: Appearance is very important. Our first king, Saul, was chosen because of his appearance.

HUSBAND: But he turned out to not be a very good king.

ESSENE: That's true.

HUSBAND: You know it bothered me when you said that I am a very handsome man.

ESSENE: I'm sorry but you are. I have a confession to make also. Like your wife, my wife has not been happy sexually with me. But it is my fault, not hers.

HUSBAND: Why is that?

ESSENE: I never had strong feelings for her.

HUSBAND: You know that sometimes I notice you staring at me in a very strange way?

ESSENE: Yes, I'm sorry about that too.

HUSBAND: Is this occasional staring at me one of the reasons why you chose me as your chief helper?

ESSENE: Yes, but you proved to be very adept at making bows and arrows, and furthermore, you have become the best long bowman in the compound.

HUSBAND: You taught me well.

ESSENE: I appreciate your saying that.

HUSBAND: Since tonight might be our last night alive, do you want to discuss further your reason for staring at me occasionally?

ESSENE: Yes and no, but more "no" than "yes."

HUSBAND: I understand. By the way, does it bother you that some Jews feel, since neither of us has any children, that we have violated the law in scripture "Be Fruitful and Multiply"?

ESSENE: I've thought about that; and I think I have an answer. Namely, God tries to communicate with man, and man writes down in scripture what he thinks God is telling him. But the words of scripture are only man's approximation of what he thinks God is saying. Isn't it presumptuous of man to feel that his choice of words for what God is saying are the ones that God would choose? Now as far as being fruitful, we have been fruitful. We have been fruitful in that we have produced for Elazar and all the people up here at Masada, the best possible bows and arrows. Also, as far as multiply is concerned, I have multiplied by training you. And if you survive tomorrow, you will multiply by training your helper, like I have trained you.

HUSBAND: Thank you for explaining that to me.

ESSENE: It is getting very late. Let us eat and drink and rest a little, so we can do what Elazar wants us to do when the Romans come through the breach tomorrow.

HUSBAND: Yes we should. I want to thank you for all the time you spent training me.

ESSENE: As a student, you might have outdone your teacher. And you are certainly better with the long bow than I am.

HUSBAND: Thank you. And God bless you.

ESSENE: And God bless you.

SCENE 8

At rise: The next evening, after the Romans have captured Masada. The Roman commander, Flavius Silva, his second in command, Tiberius Julius Alexander, and Elazar ben Yair, commander of Masada, who has been taken alive, are talking.

SILVA: (Looking at ben Yair.) All the women and children were dead when we entered the stronghold, except for the two women and five children who hid in a cave. Why was that?

BEN YAIR: The men decided to dispatch their families so that none would be taken alive and suffer your notorious Roman cruelty, like the women being repeatedly raped and then they, if they were still alive, and their children sold into slavery to work in mines somewhere and never again see the light of day.

SILVA: What else would you expect? You kept us here for three years and killed over a thousand legionnaires before we finally won.

BEN YAIR: Why did you besiege us? We were no threat to Rome.

SILVA: Masada was the last Jewish stronghold, and it was necessary for Roman honor to conquer you.

BEN YAIR: So it was necessary for us to make sure our wives and children would not fall into your clutches by dispatching them, and then all the men fight and kill as many Romans legionnaires as they could.

TIBERIUS: Well you certainly did that.

SILVA: It is interesting that Rome has had the most problems at the two furthest ends of the empire, namely Britain in the West and Judaea here in the East, and I have been called upon to fight in both places.

TIBERIUS: Because you are Rome's greatest general.

SILVA: Speaking of generals, and much as I regret the heavy toll you people took on us today, that was a magnificent defense you Jews put on.

TIBERIUS: Yes, you had a tight but expanding half-ring of swordsman around our breach in your wall and we could not get into formation and use our usual tactics, and our legionnaires were slaughtered as they came through the breach. Then when your half-ring had expanded enough under pressure that we finally could break through, your men quickly retreated in good order to the higher ground of a palace area where there were prepared stockpiles of bows and arrows as well as archers that covered the retreat; and your men's skill with the bow and arrow continued the slaughter of us Romans. I have never seen such deadly accuracy.

BEN YAIR: Well, for one, we had three years to practice while you built your ramp to get up here; and, furthermore, during the time of the Maccabees, we Jews were known as the "People of the Bow."

SILVA: I noticed that besides the men, you had some women who shot at us with the bow and arrow.

BEN YAIR: Yes, there were five women, expert as men with the bow and arrow, to be sure a little lighter bow than what the men use, except for one who was so strong she could shoot with the men's heavier bow, who indicated that they wanted to fight with the men. Although these women started out on the palace level with the archers and were not part of the original half-ring around the breach.

SILVA: Did these women have children?

BEN YAIR: Yes!

SILVA: What happened to them?

BEN YAIR: They were dispatched like all the other children.

SILVA: I noticed some men who were very young were also fighting.

BEN YAIR: Yes, when a Jewish boy becomes thirteen, there is a ceremony where he officially becomes a man. Some were allowed to fight if they were suitable.

SILVA: You Jews seem to like the bow and arrow more than the sword.

BEN YAIR: We Jews believe in using the power of our minds rather than the strength of our arms in fighting. Like everybody we started out using a sword to fight. Then we moved up to the spear so a man could kill another man, or a wild animal for that matter, at a distance. Then we developed the sling and that increased the distance a man could kill at. You probably have heard of the story of King David, a normal sized man, who killed the Philistine giant Goliath with one stone from a sling. Finally, we perfected the ultimate modern weapon, the bow and arrow, which helped us to kill so many of your legionnaires. But (Looking at Tiberius.) weren't you born Jewish, shouldn't you know all this?

TIBERIUS: Yes, I was born Jewish. In fact the famous Philo of Alexandria was my uncle and my father, his brother, was head of the Jewish community in Alexandria. But I went to Rome when I was very young and became a Roman citizen and then spent my life in the Roman army.

BEN YAIR: Weren't you procurator of Judaea for two years over two decades ago?

TIBERIUS: Yes I was.

BEN YAIR: And didn't you have two of the sons of a man named Judas the Galilean, a great religious leader, who, by the way, was a relative of mine and who was the founder of what is called the "Fourth Philosophy," and who also planted the seeds of our eventual revolt against you Romans, crucified?

TIBERIUS: Yes, I did; they were troublemakers.

BEN YAIR: Rome was bleeding us dry with taxation; we had to do something.

TIBERIUS: It is Rome's prerogative to tax subject peoples.

BEN YAIR: And also when you were Prefect of Egypt, you had two thousand Alexandrian Jews killed by the legions. What was your excuse then?

TIBERIUS: The Alexandrian Jews were being very intransigent; it was necessary to kill some to restore order.

SILVA: Enough of this! (Looking at ben Yair.) Tell me about this new form of Judaism, the "Fourth Philosophy", and where does the word "fourth" come from?

BEN YAIR: The word "fourth" comes from the fact that originally there were three types of Jews: Sadducees, Pharisees, and the Essenes. The "Fourth Philosophy" is a fourth variety sometimes called the "Fourth Way" or just "The Way". As I said before, it was founded by a man named Judas the Galilean, who besides being a religious leader was a political revolutionary and believed in expelling Rome from Judaea.

SILVA: What about the other forms of Judaism?

BEN YAIR: The Sadducees, who only accept the written law, that is to say what is written in our scriptures, and who reject the oral law, which are expansions and interpretations of the written law, were usually rich Jews in league with you Romans, who controlled the Temple, unfortunately destroyed by your army three years ago.

TIBERIUS: The Temple was destroyed by you Jews fighting amongst yourselves. Jerusalem was a strong fortress, you could have held out for many more years, what with your underground water supply and invulnerable walls. But when we Romans weren't attacking, you would fight amongst yourselves, destroying your food supplies and killing each other.

BEN YAIR: Unfortunately, we Jews are sometimes not only our own best friends but sometimes our own worst enemies.

SILVA: Yes, and don't forget that the Romans during the time of Pompey were invited to come here to

Judaea because you Jews could not resolve your own differences.

BEN YAIR: But we didn't know that you would never leave.

TIBERIUS: What did you expect?

BEN YAIR: At least a gentle rule instead of the excesses of some of your procurators.

SILVA: Enough of this arguing! (Looking at ben Yair.) Continue telling me about the other forms of Judaism.

BEN YAIR: The Pharisees are another group, very diverse and numerous. They mostly accept both the written and the oral law. The third group, the Essenes, are very otherworldly, mostly concerned with purity and avoidance of pleasure. They are mostly celibate, although some get married; but, once a wife gets pregnant, they abstain from intercourse with her to prove that the object of the marriage was not pleasure but the begetting of children. Also, they are vegetarians for the most part. In fact, the man named James, who became one of the leaders of The Way, was a vegetarian and might have started out as an Essene.

SILVA: Not to be too mundane, what is wrong with eating meat?

BEN YAIR: Our scriptures say that until the time of Noah, men were not supposed to eat meat. Something about the blood of an animal being sacred. But after the flood that occurred in Noah's time, man was allowed to eat meat, since it was felt that most men could not be vegetarians.

SILVA: Soldiers need to eat meat; it makes them strong and better fighters. But to get back to The Way, didn't it split into two groups?

BEN YAIR: Yes. After the time of Judas the Galilean, The Way split into two factions. One group was led by the aforementioned man named James, who felt that all the rules and regulations of Judaism had to be obeyed, and that you had to be first an observant Jew in order to be a follower of The Way. Also, as I may have indicated before, many of these were violently opposed to Roman rule, especially the burdensome taxation by Rome. In fact, I, and most of the people here at Masada, are or were followers of The Way.

TIBERIUS: I've heard it said that James lived to be over ninety before he died.

BEN YAIR: Not everybody believes that.

SILVA: To get back to The Way, I thought you people here at Masada were called Zealots.

BEN YAIR: Some people call us Zealots, some call us followers of The Way, and some, even, call us Sicarii, like the knife.

SILVA: You said The Way split into two groups, what about the other group?

BEN YAIR: The other group of The Way was led by a man named Paul, who felt that The Way should be for all people, even if they were not Jewish. He felt that most of the rules and regulations of traditional Judaism were not necessary to be a good person. He wanted a religion for the pagans that would make them all behave as Jews in what he felt were the important parts of Judaism, namely the morality of the Jews.

Also for this group there was an emphasis on the word "Love" and also on the concept of Salvation which I have never understood. People of this group are now called Jewish Christians. Finally, this group, contrary to the inclinations of the other group led by James, leaned in a direction of accommodation with Rome.

SILVA: I am confused by all these terms, Christian, Jewish Christian, the Fourth Philosophy, the Fourth Way, The Way, Zealots, Sicarii, and also the differences between them.

BEN YAIR: It is confusing, but the terms will eventually sort themselves out.

SILVA: I should tell you both, that surprising as it sounds, my wife in Rome has taken to this form of Judaism. Before she became a Jewish Christian, or Christian, as these people are generally called in Rome, and not to burden you both with my personal problems, she was very promiscuous, saying to me, which as you can guess made me very angry, she would not be beautiful forever and didn't want to waste any of her years of beauty. Then when she became a Christian, surprisingly, she stopped being promiscuous, and now she talks forever about spiritual love.

TIBERIUS: Speaking of promiscuity, it is also common to some Jews.

SILVA: Yes, my wife tells me that in the Jewish scriptures there is the mention of King David who was very free with his sexual favors. She tells me about the story of David and Bathsheba. It seems David saw Bathsheba bathing, naked, on her roof and was so entranced with her that he had her brought to the palace. Not unexpectedly, Bathsheba soon became pregnant, so David had her army husband, Uriah, who was away fighting on some faraway front, brought home so they could blame the pregnancy on him. But her husband would not sleep with her and stayed in the barracks because he felt that since his men were still on the front, he should not sleep with his wife. So, David, as a last resort, had her army husband sent to the most dangerous part of the front and thereby killed in battle, and then David could marry Bathsheba. Everybody blames David for this. My wife says that it was more Bathsheba's doing: she was very beautiful and knew that by bathing on her roof, naked, she would catch the eye of David and be brought to the palace. They were a perfect match: she was not happy with her unambitious low-level army officer husband and David was not happy with any of his sons from his other wives becoming king. Solomon was his second child with Bathsheba and became a great king after David died.

TIBERIUS: That is a very interesting interpretation of David and Bathsheba. I have never heard that before. But to get back to your wife, she, like Bathsheba was, is very beautiful. I have seen her in Rome. Did you ever think of divorcing her when she was being unfaithful?

SILVA: I thought of it, but I love her too much. But now I will have my revenge. Of the two women and five children here at Masada who hid in a cave until the fighting was over, one of the women is very beautiful. I am going to bring her back with me to Rome

and let my wife see what it's like to suffer the agony
of jealousy.

BEN YAIR: What will happen to the other woman and the five
children?

SILVA: I will send them to Jerusalem with some gold for
the woman to take care of the children. But we have
talked enough. I want to return to my tent and my
beautiful Jewess. Ben Yair, I will say goodbye to you.
(He leaves.)

TIBERIUS: You know, you weren't the only Jew to survive. You
and your men were very effective in killing your own
wounded so that none would be taken alive. But
there were two besides you who survived.

BEN YAIR: Yes I know about those two. What will happen to
them?

TIBERIUS: Silva tells me that Rome wants all male survivors of
Masada crucified.

BEN YAIR: Would you allow me to kill those two men quickly
with a Sicarii knife? I promise not to use it on myself.

TIBERIUS: No, Silva would be angry with me.

BEN YAIR: I thought you'd say that. Some of us Jews have a saying, "We lose the worst and we gain the best."

TIBERIUS: I was born Jewish, but I am now a Roman.

BEN YAIR: I can see that.

TIBERIUS: You think I am a terrible person because I fight for
Rome, and as procurator was responsible for the crucifixion of two of the sons of Judas the Galilean, and
also as Prefect of Egypt responsible for the massacre
of some of the Alexandrian Jews.

BEN YAIR: Yes I do.

TIBERIUS: What about the Maccabean king Alexander Jannaeus? He had 800 Pharisees impaled. And furthermore, while they were dying, he had their wives and children killed in front of them. Wasn't that worse than what I did? Also, he aligned himself with the Sadducees who eventually became Roman wards to help them keep their wealth and maintain their power over the less wealthy Jews.

BEN YAIR: As I said before, the Jews can not only be their own best friends, but sometimes their own worst enemies; and also, they are always changing sides. The king you mentioned, Alexander Jannaeus, was almost destroyed during one of the endless internecine struggles of our people, except for the fact that one group of Pharisees at a critical point came over to his side. But on his deathbed, he told his wife, the Queen, Alexandra Salome, to align herself with the Pharisees, rather than the Sadducees.

TIBERIUS: Why do you think he did this?

BEN YAIR: Either out of guilt over the slaughter of the 800 Pharisees or a realization that the Sadducees only cared about themselves and their other privileged ilk.

TIBERIUS: You know, my becoming a Roman can't be all that wrong. Many Jews become Roman citizens. Also, I must have some good qualities to have become second in command to Vespasian, who is now emperor of Rome.

BEN YAIR: And then you became second in command to his
              son, Titus, and now second in command to Silva.
              Aren't you being successively demoted?

TIBERIUS: I don't care; I have recently contracted the disease
              Leprosy which as you know is eventually fatal. But
              before we finish this conversation, there is one ques-
              tion I must ask. Why did you Jews stay up here on
              this mountaintop? You could have left and melted
              into the ordinary population and maybe all survived.

BEN YAIR: That's a good question.

TIBERIUS: Did all those people stay here because of you? You
              said before that you are related to Judas the Galilean?
              Are you his grandson and therefore, since I think
              none of his sons are alive, are you now the titular
              leader of The Way? And were all those people here
              at Masada your honor guard, and that's why they
              stayed?

BEN YAIR: Is it important for you to know?

TIBERIUS: Yes, did all these people here at Masada die because
              they were protecting you as their leader?

BEN YAIR: Do you think that I would let almost a thousand Jews
              die just to protect me? The people here at Masada
              and I, as their military leader, were protecting some-
              one else: an elderly man who was a very important
              person in The Way. I, and all these people here, were
              his honor guard. You notice that there was a separate
              group of bodies found in one of the palaces; that was
              his body and that of his family. But don't ask me any
              questions about him; I will refuse to answer.

TIBERIUS: Was he possibly Judas the Galilean, who through some convoluted plot managed to survive being crucified as supposedly he was, way back when?

BEN YAIR: I am not going to answer any questions about who he was.

TIBERIUS: All right, but I do have another question for you that I hope you will answer: which of the two groups that The Way has split into, do you personally favor?

BEN YAIR: After the deaths of the leaders of the two groups, James and Paul, I lost interest in the controversies between them and decided to let the followers of each group sort out their differences and determine which group, if any, will dominate in the future.

TIBERIUS: I have the feeling that the followers of Paul will end up being the more dominant.

BEN YAIR: It does seem that way.

BEN YAIR: So what happens now?

TIBERIUS: After the legions rest up and refit themselves, we will all go to Jerusalem. I must leave you now and attend to the legions, since, as second in command, I am in charge of logistics.

SCENE 9

At Rise: A little while after the final battle at Masada, Second and his Essene wife are living in an Essene village near Jerusalem.

ESSENE WOMAN: I feel guilty that we went down the Snake Path ourselves and did not save anybody else from Masada.

SECOND: We had no choice.

ESSENE WOMAN: I know but I still feel guilty.

SECOND: You Jews feel guilty about everything.

ESSENE WOMAN: I told you not to talk like that; you are as Jewish as any Jew. Because you said that I am not going to cohabit with you tonight.

SECOND: But we are trying to get you pregnant again.

ESSENE WOMAN: We can skip a night. Besides the people here stare at me as if I am doing something wrong by cohabiting with you so frequently; it seems in a small village like this, everybody knows everybody's business.

SECOND: No, the women stare at you because they are jealous of your beauty, and the men stare at you because they all want you, even if they are Essenes.

ESSENE WOMAN: You're probably right and you know what, we are going to have to leave this village and go to a bigger one, or a city even, where we can avoid this small village gossip.

SECOND: I am ready to go whenever you are. But that brings up something I have been meaning to talk to you about.

ESSENE WOMAN: And what is that?

SECOND: I can't get over how the people at Masada behaved compared to the Jews of Rome where I grew up.

ESSENE WOMAN: What do you mean?

SECOND: You know that even though my father was not Jewish, all our family friends were Jewish, which was my mother's doing, although my father didn't seem to complain.

ESSENE WOMAN: Was your father accepted by your mother's friends?

SECOND: At first not so much but after a while any objection to him seemed to disappear.

ESSENE WOMAN: Do you know why?

SECOND: Well for one, he was a very good man.

ESSENE WOMAN: And is there a second reason?

SECOND: Yes, he not only taught me the art of sword fighting, but any Jewish boy in the community who wanted to learn. Most of the parents of these boys were grateful for this.

ESSENE WOMAN: You were talking about the difference between the Jews at Masada and the ones in Rome.

SECOND: Yes. Most of the Jewish men I knew in Rome did not seem to be like the men at Masada, who were fighters. The Jewish men in Rome were not fighters but merchants and tradesmen.

ESSENE WOMAN: Like some of the men in the big villages and cities here in Judaea.

SECOND: Yes, but more importantly, most of the wives of these men did not seem like they would allow their husbands to put them and their children away.

ESSENE WOMAN: You mean even if they knew the alternative was a horrible death.

SECOND: They probably would not have allowed themselves to think of that.

ESSENE WOMAN: You know, even at Masada, a lot of the women had to be convinced by other women what was in store for them if their husbands did not put them away.

SECOND: So are the Jews of Rome different than the ones at Masada.

ESSENE WOMAN: The differences may be superficial. You notice how good the Jews are as merchants and tradesmen. There is a saying in Scriptures: "Whatever one puts one's hand to, one should do it with all one's might."

SECOND: Maybe that's why the Jewish community accepted my father, because he was so good as a sword fighter.

ESSENE WOMAN: The scriptural command to do what one does
with all one's might, which made Jews so good
in being merchants and tradesmen, would
have transformed them into their doing what
had to be done at Masada. Remember some
of the people at Masada were merchants and
tradesmen before they went to Masada.

SECOND: I don't see the connection.

ESSENE WOMAN: It is hard to explain.

SECOND: And what about the wives of these Jewish merchants and tradesmen? It seemed to me that
to many of the Jewish wives of Rome, the
idea of being put away by their husbands was
unthinkable. I cannot imagine many of them
accepting this. In fact, I think they would have
said, when the idea of being killed by their
husbands came up, that they would kill their
husbands rather than the other way around.

ESSENE WOMAN: The wives accepted it at Masada; and, the
Roman Jewish wives would have accepted it
also when they finally realized it was the best
possible option.

SECOND: I am glad that we escaped from Masada and I
did not have to put you and our child away.

ESSENE WOMAN: So am I.

SECOND: I'm glad that you had the physical ability to
climb down the Snake Path and the courage to
risk being caught alive by the Romans, much
as I would have tried to prevent that.

ESSENE WOMAN: There is an old saying that It takes three things to live the good life: courage, God's grace, and knowledge; but, unfortunately, you need them in that order.

SECOND: That's interesting and I certainly agree with that.

ESSENE WOMAN: Maybe we can cohabit tonight.

SECOND: Okay. But I am a little tired now.

ESSENE WOMAN: You're playing with me now, but I guess I deserve it.

SECOND: No you don't deserve it. But to get serious, I have been thinking about this for a while and have been waiting for an opportunity to tell you how grateful I am for you to have made it easy for me to go to Masada, and there become part of the fighting heart of Israel. I love you for that, as well, of course, for other reasons.

ESSENE WOMAN: I think maybe it is time for us to go to bed.

SECOND: Yes maybe it is.

SCENE 10

At Rise: Some years after what happened at Masada. Josephus, the man who wrote the book "The Jewish War", that contains the only historical account of what happened at Masada, is talking to the writer of the Gospel of Mark, which many scholars think was the first of the four Gospels (not Matthew) to be written.

MARK: So why do most Jews in Judaea and Galilee, think of you as a traitor?

JOSEPHUS: Because of what happened at Jotpata.

MARK: What did happen?

JOSEPHUS: Well, I was commander of the Zealot forces in Galilee and also commander of the garrison at Jotpata, which was our last stronghold in the Galilee.

MARK: What, you were commander of the Zealots in Galilee, but yet in your book you talk disapprovingly about the Zealots.

JOSEPHUS: In retrospect, I realized that besides certain members of The Way, the Zealots were responsible for the terrible events that occurred which led to the destruction of Jerusalem and the Temple.

MARK: War makes for strange alliances.

JOSEPHUS: That's a good way of looking at what happened.

MARK: But go on; tell me what actually happened at Jotpata.

JOSEPHUS: The Romans finally broke through our defenses and I, and about 40 of my men, hid in a cave, hoping the Romans would not find us. Well they did and they wanted us to come out of the cave and surrender.

MARK: Yes, okay, then what happened.

JOSEPHUS: The men decided to not be taken alive for fear of being crucified.

MARK: I understand; crucifixion is a terrible way to die compared to a quick death from a sword or Sicarii knife. But go on.

JOSEPHUS: I convinced the men to divide up into pairs, draw lots and one kill the other, then form new pairs and continue doing the same. This happened until finally getting down, by luck, or providence, mind you, to me and one other man. Then rather than continue with drawing lots to decide which of us two would kill the other and then the last man would kill himself, I made a pact with the other man to surrender to the Romans in the hopes that I could ingratiate myself with Vespasian, which is what happened.

MARK: What happened to the other man?

JOSEPHUS: I lost contact with him and I don't know what happened to him.

MARK: Well it seems that you were just lucky and not a traitor. I mean you did risk crucifixion, which showed a lot of courage.

JOSEPHUS: Thank you for saying that.

MARK: But tell me, as commander of rebel forces in Galilee
             and commander at Jotpata, did you ever do any-
             thing to betray the Jewish cause?

JOSEPHUS: No, I swear. All I did is save my life when all was
             lost.

MARK: Then I don't think you were a traitor, unless you did
             things in the cave that you shouldn't have, like take
             advantage of your rank.

JOSEPHUS: I might have at various times used my rank in some
             untoward way, but my survival was accomplished
             mostly by using my powers of persuasion.

MARK: Well, you did convince Vespasian to let you become
             his liaison with the Jews.

JOSEPHUS: And, in doing so, saved the lives of many Jews.

MARK: It doesn't matter that I don't think you were a traitor,
             but rather how will you be judged in the future by
             your fellow Jews.

JOSEPHUS: My book will redeem me.

MARK: But your book seems to make the Romans out to
             be good and you blame a lot of what happened in
             the Jewish War on extremist Jews. It seems obvious
             that you did this to gain favor with the Romans.
             For example, your description of what happened at
             Masada is not true. I know that you were not an eye-
             witness to what happened there; and, also, I heard
             from a legionnaire, who was actually there, the true
             story of what really happened.

JOSEPHUS: Well the emperor Vespasian had sort of adopted me
             and I had to write in such a way that didn't antago-
             nize him or his son, Titus. I couldn't very well write

how, after dispatching their wives and children, the remaining couple of hundred or so Jews were able to kill over a thousand legionnaires.

MARK: I guess you couldn't. To bring up something else you might have done wrong; I've heard that you have divorced your Jewish wife and married a young, beautiful well-connected Roman woman?

JOSEPHUS: Yes, my marriage wasn't going well and my association with Vespasian gave me access to Roman high society with its many beautiful young women. How could I resist?

MARK: I would have.

JOSEPHUS: Yes, I've heard that you Christians don't approve of divorce.

MARK: Yes we are against divorce.

JOSEPHUS: Each to his own.

MARK: But to get back to your book, why is there no mention of Jesus Christ in your book?

JOSEPHUS: I believe that he was the same man as Judas the Galilean, who is in my book.

MARK: That's ridiculous! I never heard of Judas the Galilean until I read your book and certainly don't believe that he and Jesus were the same person.

JOSEPHUS: Alright, then why in your book, or the Gospel of Mark as it is now called, is the man called Jesus made out to be more of a religious dissident rather than a political revolutionary like some people think he was?

MARK: Just as you, Josephus, have written your book to make yourself acceptable to Rome, so I, in my account, have done a similar thing to make Jesus, and Christianity in general, acceptable to Rome, by making Jesus out to be only a religious dissident and suppress any indication of his being a political revolutionary.

JOSEPHUS: Okay, I understand that. So are you saying that Christianity must be separate from Judaism to avoid Roman antagonism toward the Jews?

MARK: Yes, and furthermore, I believe as Paul does that Christianity is for all people and that the large amount of rules and regulations of the religious Jews are too onerous for new converts; and, also, in my opinion, are not necessary in order for people to do justly, be merciful, and do unto others what they would have others do unto them, which are the important essentials of Judaism that I feel Christians should adopt.

JOSEPHUS: But your account puts the blame for the death of Jesus on the Jews. This is not true. Jesus was crucified by the Romans. The Romans only crucified people who were revolutionaries. Although there were Jews like most Sadducees who disliked Jesus and were in league with the Romans against him.

MARK: Why were the Sadducees so against Jesus?

JOSEPHUS: Because Jesus objected strenuously to the profiteering money-lenders in the Temple Court, who were Sadducees, which gave them great power over the ordinary Jews and brought them much wealth through payments for obligatory sacrifices.

MARK: I see.

JOSEPHUS: But, I should ask you why is there little or no men-
             tion of the enmity of the Sadducees against Jesus in
             your account? You only write about the Pharisees as
             the enemy of Jesus, some of whom felt very favor-
             ably about Jesus.

MARK: With the destruction of the Temple, the Sadducees
             disappeared and were no longer worth writing
             about.

JOSEPHUS: Okay. There is another thing that bothers me;
             namely, that all accounts about Jesus that are writ-
             ten after yours, which is the first to be written, will
             incorporate your view that the Jews were responsi-
             ble for the death of Jesus, rather than the Romans;
             and, as Christianity spreads throughout the Roman
             Empire, as it seems it will, the antipathy of Christians
             toward Jews will increase.

MARK: That's possible, but that might be the price that
             must be paid for Christianity to survive.

JOSEPHUS: But what if this leads to outright hatred by Christians
             of Jews, even to the point of violence? How will you
             feel about that?

MARK: I repeat, just like you wrote your book to avoid your
             being censured by Rome, so have I wrote about Jesus
             to make Christianity acceptable to Rome.

JOSEPHUS: So you are saying that we have both changed his-
             tory for expediency. But, your account might do the
             Jewish people a lot more harm than mine will ever
             do. They might be forever blamed for the death of
             Jesus because of what you wrote.

MARK: I hope that you are wrong about that.

JOSEPHUS: But if I am right, it will be very bad for future Jews.

MARK: Yes, it could be. Let us hope that what I wrote doesn't bode badly for future Jews.

JOSEPHUS: I hope so too.

MARK: Time will tell.

JOSEPHUS: Yes it will.

(CURTAIN.)